CLASS OF 2022

Congrats

GRAD

CLASS OF 2022

GRAD

Congrats

GRAD

Class of 2022

Congrats GRAD — CLASS OF 2022

From: ....

I Wish You:

_____

_____

_____

_____

Always Remember:

_____

_____

_____

_____

Memory Jar
Share a favorite memory or advice.

_____

_____

_____

_____

_____

Congrats GRAD — CLASS OF 2022

From: ....

I Wish You:

_____

_____

_____

_____

Always Remember:

_____

_____

_____

_____

Memory Jar

Share a favorite memory or advice.

_____

_____

_____

_____

CLASS OF 2022

Congrats GRAD

From: ....

I Wish You:

_____

_____

_____

_____

Always Remember:

_____

_____

_____

_____

Memory Jar
Share a favorite memory or advice.

_____

_____

_____

_____

_____

_____

CLASS OF 2022

Congrats GRAD

From: ....

I Wish You:

_____

_____

_____

_____

_____

Always Remember:

_____

_____

_____

_____

Memory Jar

Share a favorite memory or advice.

_____

_____

_____

_____

_____

_____

Congrats GRAD

CLASS OF 2022

From: ....

I Wish You:

_____

_____

_____

_____

Always Remember:

_____

_____

_____

_____

Memory Jar
Share a favorite memory or advice.

_____

_____

_____

_____

_____

Congrats Grad

CLASS OF 2022

From: ....

I Wish You:

_____

_____

_____

_____

Always Remember:

_____

_____

_____

_____

Memory Jar
Share a favorite memory or advice.

_____

_____

_____

_____

_____

_____

CLASS OF 2022

Congrats **GRAD**

From: ....

I Wish You:

_____

_____

_____

_____

Always Remember:

_____

_____

_____

_____

Memory Jar
Share a favorite memory or advice.

_____

_____

_____

_____

_____

Congrats CLASS OF 2022 **GRAD**

From: ....

I Wish You:

_____
_____
_____
_____
_____

Always Remember:

_____
_____
_____
_____

Memory Jar
Share a favorite memory or advice.

_____
_____
_____
_____
_____
_____

CLASS OF 2022

Congrats **GRAD**

From: ....

I Wish You:

_____

_____

_____

_____

Always Remember:

_____

_____

_____

_____

Memory Jar

Share a favorite memory or advice.

_____

_____

_____

_____

_____

_____

CLASS OF 2022

Congrats **G R A D**

From: ....

I Wish You:

_____

_____

_____

_____

_____

Always Remember:

_____

_____

_____

_____

_____

Memory Jar
Share a favorite memory or advice.

_____

_____

_____

_____

_____

_____

_____

Congrats **CLASS OF 2022** **GRAD**

From: ....

I Wish You:

_____

_____

_____

_____

_____

Always Remember:

_____

_____

_____

_____

Memory Jar
Share a favorite memory or advice.

_____

_____

_____

_____

_____

_____

Congrats **CLASS OF 2022** **GRAD**

From: ....

I Wish You:

_____

_____

_____

_____

_____

Always Remember:

_____

_____

_____

_____

_____

Memory Jar
Share a favorite memory or advice.

_____

_____

_____

_____

_____

_____

_____

Congrats GRAD

CLASS OF 2022

From: ....

I Wish You:

_____

_____

_____

_____

_____

Always Remember:

_____

_____

_____

_____

_____

Memory Jar
Share a favorite memory or advice.

_____

_____

_____

_____

_____

_____

Congrats **CLASS OF 2022** **GRAD**

From: ....

I Wish You:

_____
_____
_____
_____
_____

Always Remember:

_____
_____
_____
_____

Memory Jar

Share a favorite memory or advice.

_____
_____
_____
_____
_____
_____

Congrats GRAD

CLASS OF 2022

From: ....

I Wish You:

_____

_____

_____

_____

Always Remember:

_____

_____

_____

_____

Memory Jar

Share a favorite memory or advice.

_____

_____

_____

_____

_____

_____

CLASS OF 2022

Congrats **GRAD**

From: ....

I Wish You:

_____

_____

_____

_____

Always Remember:

_____

_____

_____

_____

Memory Jar
Share a favorite memory or advice.

_____

_____

_____

_____

_____

_____

Congrats GRAD

CLASS OF 2022

From: ....

I Wish You:

_____

_____

_____

_____

_____

Always Remember:

_____

_____

_____

_____

Memory Jar
Share a favorite memory or advice.

_____

_____

_____

_____

_____

_____

Congrats GRAD
CLASS OF 2022

From: ....

I Wish You:

_____

_____

_____

_____

_____

Always Remember:

_____

_____

_____

_____

_____

Memory Jar

Share a favorite memory or advice.

_____

_____

_____

_____

_____

_____

_____

_____

Congrats GRAD
CLASS OF 2022

From: ....

I Wish You:

_____

_____

_____

_____

_____

Always Remember:

_____

_____

_____

_____

_____

Memory Jar
Share a favorite memory or advice.

_____

_____

_____

_____

_____

_____

_____

Congrats GRAD

CLASS OF 2022

From: ....

I Wish You:

_____

_____

_____

_____

Always Remember:

_____

_____

_____

_____

Memory Jar
Share a favorite memory or advice.

_____

_____

_____

_____

_____

Congrats GRAD

CLASS OF 2022

From: ....

I Wish You:

_____

_____

_____

_____

_____

Always Remember:

_____

_____

_____

_____

_____

Memory Jar

Share a favorite memory or advice.

_____

_____

_____

_____

_____

_____

CLASS OF 2022

Congrats **GRAD**

From: ....

I Wish You:

_____

_____

_____

_____

_____

Always Remember:

_____

_____

_____

_____

_____

Memory Jar

Share a favorite memory or advice.

_____

_____

_____

_____

_____

_____

Congrats GRAD

CLASS OF 2022

From: ....

I Wish You:

_____

_____

_____

_____

Always Remember:

_____

_____

_____

_____

Memory Jar
Share a favorite memory or advice.

_____

_____

_____

_____

_____

_____

CLASS OF 2022

Congrats GRAD

From: ....

I Wish You:

_____
_____
_____
_____
_____

Always Remember:

_____
_____
_____
_____
_____

Memory Jar

Share a favorite memory or advice.

_____
_____
_____
_____
_____
_____
_____

Congrats Grad

CLASS OF 2022

From: ....

I Wish You:

_____
_____
_____
_____
_____

Always Remember:

_____
_____
_____
_____
_____

Memory Jar
Share a favorite memory or advice.

_____
_____
_____
_____
_____
_____
_____

CLASS OF 2022

Congrats **GRAD**

From: ....

I Wish You:

_____

_____

_____

_____

Always Remember:

_____

_____

_____

_____

Memory Jar

Share a favorite memory or advice.

_____

_____

_____

_____

_____

_____

Congrats GRAD
CLASS OF 2022

From: ....

I Wish You:

_____

_____

_____

_____

Always Remember:

_____

_____

_____

_____

Memory Jar
Share a favorite memory or advice.

_____

_____

_____

_____

_____

_____

Congrats CLASS OF 2022 **GRAD**

From: ....

I Wish You:

_____

_____

_____

_____

_____

Always Remember:

_____

_____

_____

_____

_____

Memory Jar
Share a favorite memory or advice.

_____

_____

_____

_____

_____

_____

Congrats GRAD

CLASS OF 2022

From: ....

I Wish You:

_____

_____

_____

_____

Always Remember:

_____

_____

_____

_____

Memory Jar
Share a favorite memory or advice.

_____

_____

_____

_____

_____

_____

Congrats GRAD
CLASS OF 2022

From: ....

I Wish You:

_____

_____

_____

_____

_____

Always Remember:

_____

_____

_____

_____

Memory Jar
Share a favorite memory or advice.

_____

_____

_____

_____

_____

Congrats GRAD

CLASS OF 2022

From: ....

I Wish You:

_____

_____

_____

_____

Always Remember:

_____

_____

_____

_____

Memory Jar

Share a favorite memory or advice.

_____

_____

_____

_____

_____

CLASS OF 2022

Congrats **GRAD**

From: ....

I Wish You:

_____

_____

_____

_____

Always Remember:

_____

_____

_____

_____

Memory Jar

Share a favorite memory or advice.

_____

_____

_____

_____

_____

Congrats GRAD
CLASS OF 2022

From: ....

I Wish You:

_____

_____

_____

_____

Always Remember:

_____

_____

_____

_____

Memory Jar
Share a favorite memory or advice.

_____

_____

_____

_____

_____

_____

_____

CLASS OF 2022

Congrats **G R A D**

From: ....

I Wish You:

_____

_____

_____

_____

_____

Always Remember:

_____

_____

_____

_____

_____

Memory Jar

Share a favorite memory or advice.

_____

_____

_____

_____

_____

_____

Congrats Grad

CLASS OF 2022

From: ....

I Wish You:

_____

_____

_____

_____

Always Remember:

_____

_____

_____

_____

Memory Jar
Share a favorite memory or advice.

_____

_____

_____

_____

_____

_____

Congrats Grad

CLASS OF 2022

From: ....

I Wish You:

_____

_____

_____

_____

_____

Always Remember:

_____

_____

_____

_____

Memory Jar

Share a favorite memory or advice.

_____

_____

_____

_____

_____

Congrats GRAD

CLASS OF 2022

From: ....

I Wish You:

_____

_____

_____

_____

Always Remember:

_____

_____

_____

_____

Memory Jar
Share a favorite memory or advice.

_____

_____

_____

_____

_____

_____

CLASS OF 2022

Congrats **GRAD**

From: ....

I Wish You:

_____

_____

_____

_____

_____

Always Remember:

_____

_____

_____

_____

_____

Memory Jar

Share a favorite memory or advice.

_____

_____

_____

_____

_____

Congrats GRAD
CLASS OF 2022

From: ....

I Wish You:

_____

_____

_____

_____

_____

Always Remember:

_____

_____

_____

_____

Memory Jar
Share a favorite memory or advice.

_____

_____

_____

_____

_____

_____

Congrats **CLASS OF 2022** **GRAD**

From: ....

I Wish You:

_____
_____
_____
_____
_____

Always Remember:

_____
_____
_____
_____
_____

Memory Jar
Share a favorite memory or advice.

_____
_____
_____
_____
_____
_____

Congrats GRAD

CLASS OF 2022

From: ....

I Wish You:

_____

_____

_____

_____

_____

Always Remember:

_____

_____

_____

_____

Memory Jar

Share a favorite memory or advice.

_____

_____

_____

_____

_____

_____

_____

CLASS OF 2022

Congrats GRAD

From: ....

I Wish You:

_____

_____

_____

_____

_____

Always Remember:

_____

_____

_____

_____

_____

Memory Jar
Share a favorite memory or advice.

_____

_____

_____

_____

_____

_____

Congrats GRAD

CLASS OF 2022

From: ....

I Wish You:

_____

_____

_____

_____

Always Remember:

_____

_____

_____

_____

Memory Jar
Share a favorite memory or advice.

_____

_____

_____

_____

_____

CLASS OF 2022

Congrats **G R A D**

From: ....

I Wish You:

_____

_____

_____

_____

_____

Always Remember:

_____

_____

_____

_____

_____

Memory Jar
Share a favorite memory or advice.

_____

_____

_____

_____

_____

Congrats **CLASS OF 2022** **GRAD**

From: ....

I Wish You:

_____

_____

_____

_____

_____

Always Remember:

_____

_____

_____

_____

_____

Memory Jar

Share a favorite memory or advice.

_____

_____

_____

_____

_____

_____

CLASS OF 2022

Congrats GRAD

From: ....

I Wish You:

_____

_____

_____

_____

_____

Always Remember:

_____

_____

_____

_____

_____

Memory Jar

Share a favorite memory or advice.

_____

_____

_____

_____

_____

_____

Congrats GRAD

CLASS OF 2022

From: ....

I Wish You:

_____

_____

_____

_____

_____

Always Remember:

_____

_____

_____

_____

Memory Jar
Share a favorite memory or advice.

_____

_____

_____

_____

_____

_____

CLASS OF 2022

Congrats GRAD

From: ....

I Wish You:

_____

_____

_____

_____

_____

Always Remember:

_____

_____

_____

_____

_____

Memory Jar
Share a favorite memory or advice.

_____

_____

_____

_____

_____

_____

Congrats CLASS OF 2022 GRAD

From: ....

I Wish You:

_____

_____

_____

_____

_____

Always Remember:

_____

_____

_____

_____

_____

Memory Jar

Share a favorite memory or advice.

_____

_____

_____

_____

_____

_____

CLASS OF 2022

Congrats GRAD

From: ....

I Wish You:

_____

_____

_____

_____

_____

Always Remember:

_____

_____

_____

_____

_____

Memory Jar

Share a favorite memory or advice.

_____

_____

_____

_____

_____

CLASS OF 2022

Congrats **G R A D**

From: ....

I Wish You:

_____
_____
_____
_____

Always Remember:

_____
_____
_____
_____

Memory Jar
Share a favorite memory or advice.

_____
_____
_____
_____
_____

CLASS OF 2022

Congrats GRAD

From: ....

I Wish You:

_____

_____

_____

_____

_____

Always Remember:

_____

_____

_____

_____

_____

Memory Jar

Share a favorite memory or advice.

_____

_____

_____

_____

_____

Congrats GRAD

CLASS OF 2022

From: ....

I Wish You:

_____

_____

_____

_____

_____

Always Remember:

_____

_____

_____

_____

Memory Jar

Share a favorite memory or advice.

_____

_____

_____

_____

_____

Congrats GRAD — CLASS OF 2022

From: ....

I Wish You:

_____

_____

_____

_____

_____

Always Remember:

_____

_____

_____

_____

Memory Jar
Share a favorite memory or advice.

_____

_____

_____

_____

_____

_____

CLASS OF 2022

Congrats **G R A D**

From: ....

I Wish You:

_____

_____

_____

_____

Always Remember:

_____

_____

_____

_____

Memory Jar

Share a favorite memory or advice.

_____

_____

_____

_____

_____

Congrats CLASS OF 2022 GRAD

From: ....

I Wish You:

_____

_____

_____

_____

Always Remember:

_____

_____

_____

_____

Memory Jar

Share a favorite memory or advice.

_____

_____

_____

_____

_____

_____

Congrats GRAD

CLASS OF 2022

From: ....

I Wish You:

_____

_____

_____

_____

Always Remember:

_____

_____

_____

_____

Memory Jar
Share a favorite memory or advice.

_____

_____

_____

_____

_____

_____

Congrats GRAD

CLASS OF 2022

From: ....

I Wish You:

_____

_____

_____

_____

Always Remember:

_____

_____

_____

_____

Memory Jar

Share a favorite memory or advice.

_____

_____

_____

_____

_____

_____

Congrats GRAD
CLASS OF 2022

From: ....

I Wish You:

_____

_____

_____

_____

_____

Always Remember:

_____

_____

_____

_____

_____

Memory Jar
Share a favorite memory or advice.

_____

_____

_____

_____

_____

_____

Congrats GRAD

CLASS OF 2022

From: ....

I Wish You:

_____

_____

_____

_____

_____

Always Remember:

_____

_____

_____

_____

Memory Jar
Share a favorite memory or advice.

_____

_____

_____

_____

_____

_____

Congrats CLASS OF 2022 **GRAD**

From: ....

I Wish You:

_____
_____
_____
_____

Always Remember:

_____
_____
_____
_____

Memory Jar
Share a favorite memory or advice.

_____
_____
_____
_____
_____

Congrats GRAD — CLASS OF 2022

From: ....

I Wish You:

_____

_____

_____

_____

_____

Always Remember:

_____

_____

_____

_____

_____

Memory Jar
Share a favorite memory or advice.

_____

_____

_____

_____

_____

Congrats CLASS OF 2022 **GRAD**

From: ....

I Wish You:

_____

_____

_____

_____

_____

Always Remember:

_____

_____

_____

_____

_____

Memory Jar

Share a favorite memory or advice.

_____

_____

_____

_____

_____

_____

Congrats GRAD — CLASS OF 2022

From: ....

I Wish You:

_____

_____

_____

_____

_____

Always Remember:

_____

_____

_____

_____

Memory Jar
Share a favorite memory or advice.

_____

_____

_____

_____

_____

_____

Congrats GRAD

CLASS OF 2022

From: ....

I Wish You:

_____

_____

_____

_____

_____

Always Remember:

_____

_____

_____

_____

Memory Jar

Share a favorite memory or advice.

_____

_____

_____

_____

_____

_____

Congrats GRAD

CLASS OF 2022

From: ....

I Wish You:

_____

_____

_____

_____

Always Remember:

_____

_____

_____

_____

Memory Jar
Share a favorite memory or advice.

_____

_____

_____

_____

_____

CLASS OF 2022

Congrats **G R A D**

From: ....

I Wish You:

_____

_____

_____

_____

_____

Always Remember:

_____

_____

_____

_____

_____

Memory Jar
Share a favorite memory or advice.

_____

_____

_____

_____

_____

_____

_____

Congrats GRAD
CLASS OF 2022

From: ....

I Wish You:

_____

_____

_____

_____

_____

Always Remember:

_____

_____

_____

_____

_____

Memory Jar
Share a favorite memory or advice.

_____

_____

_____

_____

_____

Congrats GRAD
CLASS OF 2022

From: ....

I Wish You:

_____

_____

_____

_____

_____

Always Remember:

_____

_____

_____

_____

_____

Memory Jar

Share a favorite memory or advice.

_____

_____

_____

_____

_____

Congrats GRAD — CLASS OF 2022

From: ....

I Wish You:

_____

_____

_____

_____

_____

Always Remember:

_____

_____

_____

_____

_____

Memory Jar

Share a favorite memory or advice.

_____

_____

_____

_____

_____

CLASS OF 2022

Congrats **GRAD**

From: ....

I Wish You:

_____

_____

_____

_____

Always Remember:

_____

_____

_____

_____

Memory Jar

Share a favorite memory or advice.

_____

_____

_____

_____

_____

CLASS OF 2022

Congrats **GRAD**

From: ....

I Wish You:

_____

_____

_____

_____

_____

Always Remember:

_____

_____

_____

_____

_____

Memory Jar

Share a favorite memory or advice.

_____

_____

_____

_____

_____

_____

Congrats GRAD

CLASS OF 2022

From: ....

I Wish You:

_____

_____

_____

_____

_____

Always Remember:

_____

_____

_____

_____

_____

Memory Jar
Share a favorite memory or advice.

_____

_____

_____

_____

_____

_____

CLASS OF 2022

Congrats **G R A D**

From: ....

I Wish You:

_____

_____

_____

_____

_____

Always Remember:

_____

_____

_____

_____

_____

Memory Jar

Share a favorite memory or advice.

_____

_____

_____

_____

_____

_____

_____

Congrats GRAD

CLASS OF 2022

From: ....

I Wish You:

_____
_____
_____
_____

Always Remember:

_____
_____
_____
_____

Memory Jar

Share a favorite memory or advice.

_____
_____
_____
_____
_____

Congrats Grad

CLASS OF 2022

From: ....

I Wish You:

_____

_____

_____

_____

Always Remember:

_____

_____

_____

_____

Memory Jar
Share a favorite memory or advice.

_____

_____

_____

_____

_____

Congrats GRAD

CLASS OF 2022

From: ....

I Wish You:

_____
_____
_____
_____

Always Remember:

_____
_____
_____
_____
_____

Memory Jar
Share a favorite memory or advice.

_____
_____
_____
_____
_____

CLASS OF 2022

Congrats **GRAD**

From: ....

I Wish You:

_____

_____

_____

_____

_____

Always Remember:

_____

_____

_____

_____

Memory Jar

Share a favorite memory or advice.

_____

_____

_____

_____

_____

_____

Congrats GRAD

CLASS OF 2022

From: ....

I Wish You:

_____

_____

_____

_____

Always Remember:

_____

_____

_____

_____

Memory Jar

Share a favorite memory or advice.

_____

_____

_____

_____

_____

Congrats **CLASS OF 2022** **GRAD**

From: ....

I Wish You:

_____
_____
_____
_____
_____

Always Remember:

_____
_____
_____
_____

Memory Jar

Share a favorite memory or advice.

_____
_____
_____
_____
_____

Congrats GRAD

CLASS OF 2022

From: ....

I Wish You:

_____

_____

_____

_____

_____

Always Remember:

_____

_____

_____

_____

Memory Jar

Share a favorite memory or advice.

_____

_____

_____

_____

_____

CLASS OF 2022

GRAD

CLASS OF 2022

GRAD

CLASS OF 2022

GRAD

CLASS OF 2022

GRAD

CLASS OF 2022

GRAD

CLASS OF 2022

GRAD

CLASS OF 2022

GRAD

CLASS OF 2022

GRAD

CLASS OF 2022

GRAD

CLASS OF 2022

GRAD

Congrats

GRAD

Class of 2022

Made in the USA
Monee, IL
25 May 2022

97012499R00059